# Repent of Visiting Evil Altars

by Dr. Marlene Miles

Freshwater Press 2024

freshwaterpress9@gmail.com

ISBN: 978-1-963164-66-4

Paperback Version

# Table of Contents

# Repent of Visiting Evil Altars

*Freshwater*

# It Wasn't Me

It is so hard for us to see or admit when we have done something wrong. It may be equally as tough or even more difficult to admit that our parents have done something wrong. It takes a lot of grace and maturity to look at our parents as people and evaluate, without being disrespectful or too judgey if they have done something incorrectly, especially something spiritually wrong.

Of course, there are some kids who are looking to accuse their parents of almost anything, but I believe I am chiefly talking to people who, as children, have been raised right, in the fear and the admonition of the Lord. I am not speaking expressly to children whose parents have befriended them and made them a friend instead of keeping them as a child and bringing them up in the Lord--, training them up in the way they should go.

The problem with humans, and especially some parents, is that we may get so self-righteous that we may deceive ourselves. In their endeavor to set a good example for their children, some parents can be so worried, even afraid that their child will misstep that they take things too far into holiness. These parents may try to represent holiness that they want their children to follow, but they themselves may not have attained to. Some want to display this piety and piousness when they may have been hell-raisers themselves.

Some parents, who mean no harm, have made a decision to model the correct behavior for their children who may have been just born, or when the children have reached a certain age, the parents become born-again, self-proclaimed *saints*. Really?

The issues arise though when these parents haven't properly repented themselves for all the hell raising, they have done. It is even more difficult when a parent has not been a hell-raiser, but has made some mistakes in life, even simple mistakes and has not **repented properly** to God.

If full and complete repentance has not been made to the Lord, then the iniquity for those mistakes and sins remain.

There is a certain permanence to the things we do. In writing, and on paper, one can erase an error that is made in pencil. One can erase *some* inked-in errors. Some inkpen ink cannot be erased, and tattoo ink on the body takes a lot of work to remove, else it also remains. Markers--, forget about it--, it will remain.

In speaking, most of us think we can say anything we want and then *un*speak it, say, *I'm sorry*, or *My bad*, and it is undone. But is it? The words we speak are spirit and they are life, so unless properly renounced the effects of having spoken those words will remain, possibly into perpetuity.

Errors made in blood? They are the hardest to remove and seem indelible like tattoos, but for Jesus Christ. Errors made in blood cannot be expunged, except by Jesus Christ.

*Wait, an error made in blood? How is that done? When is that done?*

It is done any time blood is spilled, knowingly and unknowingly. It is done anytime an evil covenant is made. **Covenants are made in blood, and covenants are designed to remain**. God hates broken covenant and respects covenants He makes, as well as covenants made by His people. God respects this, even if humans end up making evil covenants.

Your toddler with a crayon or marker writing on the walls of your house is one thing, but when so-called adults who should know better are recklessly going through life making contracts and covenants with their own precious blood, that's another whole thing. Some crayons are now washable from walls. The Magic Eraser sponge can work wonders in housekeeping, but have most even considered that they are writing on the walls of their bloodline and also at the same time on the walls of Time against their family's bloodline when they decide to go out into the world and color outside the lines with their own blood.

Yes, this sounds graphic because it is dire. When you sin, it is as though you take your own blood and draw or sign evil covenants that plain soap and water and perhaps not even one wash, or saying, *I didn't mean it*, or *My bad*, will get out.

**Blood is permanent.**

Unless there is Jesus.

Seriously, none of us really know all of what our parents and ancestors have signed us up for, spiritually speaking. They may not have even known, but we suffer the fallout. We have got to be very prayerful and walk circumspectly, always.

## Covenants

Oh, we'd better talk about covenants right now. What is a covenant?

A covenant is an agreement between at least two people. Often one is the weaker and the other the stronger; the weaker benefits the most from being in the covenant. It's like when your dad puts your name on his credit card account and you suddenly inherit his credit history as if you were the person who had that credit card all the time, but you don't even have one credit card or a credit rating yet. Dad is trying to help you.

The stronger is ministering to the lesser. Covenants are cut, which means if a human is cut blood will issue forth. There is not always blood, sometimes instruments in writing indicate covenant. A *covenant* is created by deed in writing, sealed and executed; or it may be implied in the contract. But even in the olden days, those documents were sealed with an official wax seal which most often was red--, like blood.

God is gracious enough to make covenant with man and we should appreciate that. God gave Noah the rainbow sign, that was a covenant made with man that the Flood would not be repeated against man in judgment. Of course, man has a responsibility in this covenant, to behave himself in obedience and godliness.

Types of covenants are covenants of works, as above; it is Old Testament. There is a Covenant of Grace, where God saves us if we believe in Jesus Christ and receive Him as the Lord and Savior of our lives. The condition is that man shall believe in Christ so that he may be saved. This is the New Testament Covenant.

The *covenant* of redemption, is the mutual agreement between the Father and Son, respecting the redemption of sinners by Christ.

Men make covenants with one another—marriage comes to mind. Kings and tribes in the bible made covenants with one another usually to make peace, keep peace, or unite together to take out a larger adversary.

In making covenant, especially in marriages, God, the presence of God is invoked as a witness to the making and ratifying of a covenant.

Money represents a person's life--, their blood. So, when money is paid to people who do things for you, or you for them, a covenant is created. If the things they do are evil, then an evil covenant is formed. Money, and things that represent money can ratify covenants.

Familywise and bloodline wise when you were born your parents and ancestors had already signed your name on their spiritual credit card account and everything they had already charged, that was yet unpaid for, **you** already and automatically owe. You now have the same credit rating in the spirit as your parents and ancestors as soon as you are born.

How can this be?

Life is spiritual and some things are super spiritual and cannot be paid for in the natural. Like ever. At least not by a human even though a human entered himself and his family into an evil covenant.

What you inherit from your parents and ancestors can be good, or it can be bad. As you live and grow spiritually, you will find out.

Sorry.

Most likely your parents and ancestors were not trying to hurt you, but they were probably trying to help themselves and their situations not knowing or considering that TIME was built into their coloring, drawing, painting, or signing with their own blood. If they thought they were doing something good for themselves, then they thought they were helping their future as well. They could have been totally wrong, but unless they will full blown witches or occultic, and just didn't care about anybody but themselves, they probably thought they were doing a good thing.

Which makes me realize right now that the breath of God is in all of us who are living; it is borrowed. In much the same way, the blood in our bodies is passed down from generation to generation in our family line--, all of us borrowing it for the volume of the book where it is written of us.

When you borrow something, you take good care of it, clean it, and return it as you found it, or even better than when you found it. You don't abuse it or use it recklessly. *Do you?*

Years ago, in college, a girlfriend of mine borrowed a dress for a special occasion. Months and months later, after my having asked her over and again, she finally returned the dress. It was on a hanger and in a dry cleaner's plastic, but the dress was shrunk down to about the size of a blouse and completely unusable. Obviously, she had washed the dress, instead of dry cleaning it, shrunken it and for months didn't know how to return it to me and save face. Her lie of placing it on a hanger and in a dry cleaner's plastic was her silent way of not taking the blame for destroying this particular dress.

She said nothing to me since, not even an attempt at an apology.

I've learned. I don't lend clothes out anymore.

We don't have a choice not to be a borrower, sharer or lender of **blood**, but we must do our part, and do our best to not abuse the blood or the authority and power in it by entering into evil contracts and covenants.

# It Is Understood

While I did not have prior knowledge that if I lent that dress to my friend that she would destroy it, it is understood that if you visit an evil altar, you are going there to make a covenant. Sinners know, if you go to a man's hotel room at 3:00 am that you are going there for a particular reason. It. Is. Understood. You are going there to sin. That hotel room, that bed, that person you are going to meet, those may all be altars. **You** may even be an altar yourself.

There is at least one altar in that room. If there is more than one, the strongest altar will prevail. The weaker will be subjected to the stronger. Maybe you two are meeting up to see who can get the most worship out of the other one. One of those altars will get the worship, the other may be the sacrifice. Don't go, but if you do, pray it is not you who is the sacrifice.

Yet, if you are going to sin --, who exactly would you be praying *to*?

If you go to a doctor's office, it is to be seen and treated medically. If you go to a dentist's office, it is to be seen and treated for some dental reason. These things are implied, and they are *understood*.

If you go to an evil altar, it is not a sightseeing tour, it is understood that you are going there to make a covenant of some kind.

Now, will the covenant be made? Will it be agreed upon, accepted, and ratified? Most likely. Witches, wizards and the like are very adept at closing deals. If they get a customer to come through the door, they intend to close that deal. Going there and bringing money, anything else requested, or anything of value seals the deal at an evil altar. It constitutes agreement and ratifies evil covenant.

Have you been to an evil altar, for any reason? This book is about how to repent.

Have you been to an evil altar on purpose, or unintentionally? There are so many kinds of altars, and they may be hidden or in plain sight. No matter what kind, marine, astral, crossroads, tree, grove, human, animal, or mobile; if the altar is not a Godly altar, it is evil.

This is what happened if you went to an evil altar, a *familiar spirit* was assigned to you and followed you home. Not just home, that *familiar spirit* now follows you everywhere. In some cultures, it is called a *follow-follow spirit*. Not only that, but they also followed you into your generations unless you renounce and denounce and repent of having gone to that evil altar, entering into some agreement with the witch, warlock, priest, or priestess there. Most people don't do this because this *following spirit* is invisible, and who knows it's there? Who even thinks they did anything wrong?

At least, at first.

A *familiar spirit* is assigned to you as soon as you go to that evil altar. You could say it marries you, but it now goes wherever you go. It also can be called a *monitoring spirit*, but you were assigned it at the evil altar. Tag, you're it. You're it because you've made a deal with the dark kingdom. Even if you gave them money or whatever they told you to bring, you now owe them because you can never pay the devil back for anything. You are now, as far as the devil is concerned, their property and they plan to get everything from you. If you don't pay up--, and you really can't then that *spirit* is like a spy to report back as to how and when is the best time to steal from you, kill and, or destroy you.

You're being tailed now, followed. A *familiar spirit* or a *monitoring spirit* reports to the hit men of the kingdom of darkness. The hitmen are the enforcers of evil covenants and curses. And their assignment is to wreck your life by stealing, killing, and destroying.

No, not stealing from, killing and destroying *other people*, which may have been your evil wish for going to the evil altar. These demonic hitmen will turn on the person who went to the altar eventually. The only way to stave them off for a while is to keep paying them, giving them what they ask for and those things asked for will escalate as time goes on as they are greedy and will ask for more and more. This doesn't just span your lifetime, but when the deal is forgotten and not passed on into the visitor's generations, the children and *children's* children start feeling the pain of the demons that great-great somebody in their family contracted with who is no longer getting worship or pay.

Think of a firing squad--, that altar that your blood relative may have gone to and asked to shoot his own enemy has now turned on your own family line and your family is getting it left and right, day after day.

*What have your ancestors done?*

You don't know unless the Holy Spirit tells you. But if your ancestors were upright, perfect, and sin-free, they are the only ones in this world, since all have sinned and fallen short.

So don't deceive yourself. You have much spiritual work to do.

If you've been one to ask yourself, why are you going through when you didn't do anything to deserve the bad stuff that seems to happen to you in your life.

Part or all of the answer may be that you've got spiritual gangsters on your tail that have come to steal, kill, and destroy. Well, these demons may be out to deconstruct the good life you want to build and live unless you've repented for your parents and grandparents.

Built into that repentance for your forefathers is that you, yourself have also forgiven them. It's part of that forgiving 70 times 7 that we humans are to do.

Then came Peter to him, and said, Lord, how oft shall my brother sin against me, and I forgive him? till seven times?

Jesus saith unto him, I say not unto thee, Until seven times: but, Until seventy times seven.
(Matthew 18:21-22)

It's in the Lord's prayer, and it is a power that the Lord gives to us to be able to do exactly as He has asked us to do.

And forgive us our debts, as we forgive our debtors. And lead us not into temptation, but deliver us from evil: For thine is the kingdom, and the power, and the glory, for ever. Amen.
(Matthew 6:12-13)

If you forgive anyone's sins, they are forgiven. If you do not forgive them, they are not forgiven. (John 20:23)

# You Didn't Go There, *Did You*?

*Go where?*

To an evil altar.

How can you know that you went to an evil altar? The clues could be right in front of you. The place is spooky, creepy, has demonic or satanic symbols and artifacts on a table, on the wall, or strewn about the place. Looks witchy. Looks occultic or even New Age-y. Is hidden or tucked away. Or the person who greets you there has a witchy or *warlocky* vibe. If you don't have the Holy Spirit, or you've turned off Holy Spirit notifications because you knew where you were going, and why, you may not pick up on any of that. Especially if there is also a Holy Bible displayed somewhere in that set up.

*A Holy Bible?*

Oh yeah, that Bible is not only to deceive the people who come in there, it is used by the person when they get scared out of their own wits for going too far into the dark world of demons and then realize they are in too deep, and the demons are out of control.

25

Yes, they have the nerve to call on God. In this way, many believe they are cleverly straddling both the kingdom of darkness and the Kingdom of Light.

They are not.

God is Merciful but He will not always strive with man. God is most likely dealing according to the grace of: *Forgive them they don't know what they do.* They may not know what they are doing, at first, but once they are hardened in this occultism, they may look for God, but they won't find Him. God is not playing, folks.

Another way you can know that you went to an evil altar is by the way the person behind the charms, crystal ball, or what have you speaks. They may say the word, *god,* but what "*god*" are they talking about?

Will they say Jesus Christ, or allude to Jesus in His Lordship or Messiahship at all? Will they say the Blood of Jesus? You may not be listening for those words, because you may already know you didn't come expecting to hear those words. If you came expecting a quick fix, or to organize or send a quick hit on someone, or to send an evil arrow to your arch nemesis, then don't pretend that you don't know where you are when you are at an evil altar.

You may not have known that you went to one, but maybe you did.

Maybe one came to you; perhaps an evil altar came to you. There are mobile altars, since people can both carry altars, and *be* altars. Some people's celebrity status is so intense, and even their purpose in life and their livelihood is dependent on them being worshipped.

*Really?*

Idolized.

*Really? Such as?*

Such as most celebrities you see on TV and in the movies. If they are not idolized and adored who will buy their records, or go to their concerts? What is a concert stage? Is it an altar? You tell me.

An altar is where the physical interfaces with the spiritual. It is a place of worship. It is a place of sacrifice.

You tell me what happens at a rock or other concert. If you are idolizing the band and or the singer, is the stage not an altar? If the singer is "channeling" their "muse" or whatever *god* they get their sounds, songs, and beats from, is that not the physical interfacing with the spirit realm? Did you spend money and now time and attention on this show?

Is this not an altar? Is this altar to Jehovah God? If not, then it is an evil altar.

Make sure **you** are not an altar, demanding worship from a person or people.

A man in his new bridegroom enthusiasm told his new wife that he worships her. She scolded him, not wanting to get into any trouble with God, she said, *"See that you do it not."*

He became perturbed with her and that was the end of the marriage. (I don't make this stuff up.)

And I John saw these things, and heard them. And when I had heard and seen, I fell down to worship before the feet of the angel which shewed me these things.

Then saith he unto me, See thou do it not: for I am thy fellowservant, and of thy brethren the prophets, and of them which keep the sayings of this book: worship God.
(Revelations 22:8-9)

We don't worship people. We don't worship angels. We don't worship things; we worship God. Mind the words of the Angel: **Worship God.**

Careful of people who worship you, or feign worship, they are usually after something from you. Beware of flattery, the Word says.

...a flattering mouth worketh ruin
(Proverbs 26:28b)

# Common Altars

Water Altars are found in various bodies of water. Rivers, themselves can be altars. Look at how many bodies of water draw sun bathers and water sport enthusiasts. As far as the water is concerned, that's worship.

Man will worship almost anything and will worship at anything. Things that supply needs for life for a man are subject to worship, especially if they ebb or flow. Part of idolatry is having to please the *god* of a place or of an element so the river, or sun, for example will keep prospering that man. So, the idolater believes that if they worship this entity the flow of the water will resume, or the sun will continue to shine to grow the crops. A river is one such thing that ebbs and flows and that can affect the productivity of businesses and harvests that depend on water and rivers. Whatever will give a man money--, if he worships money, he will worship what he believes is the source of that money as well.

Have you noticed most cities are built beside or near rivers and bodies of water? There's a reason for that: commerce. There will be an ease for ships to come in and out of port and transport goods for sale and bring in needed items from other places. The water? The devil behaves as if he has the lease on Earth, but man does. Anyway, the devil requires a *pay to play* if you want to use "his" waterways. The only way you can override this is to be in Christ--, all the way in.

Man has found out that *marine spirits* are in rivers and waters, so a river is a place that men from Pharoah up to now will go to worship, or to ask questions, get answers from things of the sea, or the entities in the water.

In this way bodies of water can be evil altars.

Jesus said, ***In that day, ask the Father anything in My Name and He will do it for you.*** This clearly means that Christians don't get things, stuff, and even inheritance from evil *spirits* or evil forces, but from God, and God alone.

Once you get into cahoots with these altars, there's no simple way to extricate yourself from them--, they believe they own you, if not perpetually at least to the 3rd or 4th generation of those who Love God. They own you and your family to the 10th generation, or more if you do not profess salvation in Jesus Christ.

The only way out of these evil covenants and to take authority over these altars you must be in Christ, all the way in, and mean it. Pay to play doesn't stop; you won't ever pay them off. On your own you cannot outsmart them. Whatever you think the contract is, is not what it really is. The devil is famous for fine print, fine-fine print, and covenants within covenants.

The childhood story of the troll that lived under a bridge and exacted toll of anyone who crossed the bridge seems to be far more than a fairytale now that we know so much more, spiritually. There is not just water and fish in that water under that bridge.

Some bodies of water demand and receive sacrifices. If you think of the mysterious and unusual deaths regarding certain bodies of water, it is sobering. There is a lake in Georgia, USA named Lake Lanier. This lake was built sometime after World War II, named after a Confederate soldier-poet, Sidney Lanier who wrote a poem about the lake.

This body of water is a huge 38,000-acre lake in northern Georgia, spanning four counties. It is infamous for a high number of deaths in it, from boating accidents, drownings, to cars mysteriously sliding off the road and killing the passengers in a sinking or sunken vehicle. There is a story of one man who jumped into that lake and was electrocuted to death. This haunted lake still attracts millions of visitors annually.

Over the years hundreds of people have died there; it is one of the deadliest lakes in the USA. The worst was Christmas 1964 when a driver, while crossing a bridge lost control of their car, and flipped into the lake killing all seven people that were in that vehicle by drowning.

Looks like folk are either not all in Christ, or are not paying that lake to "play." That evil lake appears to be taking sacrifice at will.

One day the leaders of the town of Jericho visited Elisha. "We have a problem, my lord," they told him. "This town is located in pleasant surroundings, as you can see. But the water is bad, and the land is unproductive."

Elisha said, "Bring me a new bowl with salt in it." So they brought it to him. Then he went out to the spring that supplied the town with water and threw the salt into it. And he said, "This is what the LORD says: I have purified this water. It will no longer cause death or infertility." And the water has remained pure ever since, just as Elisha said.
(2 Kings 2:19-22)

God can heal the waters of even Lake Lanier, but has anyone or any people ever asked Him? It may take a delegation, an *ecclesia* to accomplish this. Territorial *spirits*, principalities, and water altars are not to be toyed with. They are serious and they are powerful.

There is a family in another city who lost every one of their five children at different times, to the ocean, in their hometown. The ocean took five kids from one family over some years, and all the children could swim.

There are so many reports of people who barely turn their head for a moment and their child is swept away to sea. Folks, those are sacrifices. I'm not counting alligators or other animals that grab people and take them under. I'm speaking of when there appears to be nothing there but water and its undercurrent that comes up and grabs a soul for sacrifice.

And, no, I am not saying the parent made the sacrifice, but some evil entity took a person or some people because it thought it was owed, or someone nominated another as a candidate for sacrifice and there was no prayer covering or spiritual protection on that person, so they became a victim. They became prey for the kingdom of darkness. Yes, it is the parent's responsibility to cover their child in prayer at least until the age of accountability, or maturity when they can pray for themselves.

During the 1600's millions of lives were given to or taken by the sea in the Middle Passage. Those slave traders were paying to *play*, you won't convince me otherwise.

Even now, according to the World Health Organization 236,000 people drown every year, worldwide. 90% of those deaths (212,400) occur in rivers, lakes, wells, swimming pools, and water holding tanks. Drowning is the #1 cause of death for children ages 5 to 14 years old.

The Earth is approximately 70% water, and it seems the waters, rather what is *in* the water wants blood. Anything, anyone who demands blood is an altar.

Covenants can be made at any altar. Godly covenants can only be made at Godly altars. Evil covenants are made at evil altars. **Do not be reckless or careless with your blood at evil altars.** Remember, your blood also carries TIME and your blood is the blood of your children, and your *children's* children and you have the ability to sign them up for stuff. Good or bad, you can by virtue of being alive, born on Earth, and human, with blood, you can use or misuse your blood to write indelibly on the walls of your own DNA which you will pass down to your generations.

You do this at altars and by forming covenants. When a covenant is made with an idol *god* and it is not being fulfilled, the idol rages and demands payment. That payment could be money, blood, or both.

An evil covenant must be in place at Lake Lanier, and it, or whatever is in it seems to be alive to kill. But still, for some reason it has the allure to attract more than 10 million people each year to worship it.

## Astral Altars

Witches, wizards and occultic masters work with astral altars. People, nobody is playing when it comes to spiritual matters. All other altars that will be mentioned in this book are subject to the river (water or marine) altars and the astral altars; they are running the altars game.

Astral altar agents are the folks who deal with the Triangular Powers and other celestial powers, the sun, moon, stars, planets, and other powers in the galaxies.

These human agents live their lives as normal people, even highly respected people and few if any know, or can tell that they are occultic or high ranking occultic agents. If you tried to tell someone that one of these well-respected, and probably very rich people are into astral altars, they would look at you as if *you* are crazy.

Oh, saints of God, it will be very difficult to know if you've dealt with one of these people unless the Holy Spirit tells you because they are very discreet and know how to present themselves well to the public. They are occultic and that means *hidden*; and that is the way they want it.

These people are kingmakers and those that they put in authority do their bidding. They put political people in power and those people are then subject to them. This is why I no longer fret over who is in public or elected office, yet the Word says to pray for them. Whomever is in office is subject to these powers that, in a perfect world should be Jehovah God, but most often it is not. **So why we expect elected officials to behave as if they are serving the Most High God is beyond the understanding of this writer.** Even if they go to church while running for office, or once in a while for sound bites, people take on the nature of the idols in their lives, in their souls.

It is those people who have been *"put"* in positions of power who have learned how to go along to get along.

Because things aren't really what they seem, this is why those who are vocal and speak out against "authority" are treated the way that they are. The demon ruling them doesn't like that and will punish the dissident ones, somehow and at some time. Even if you believe you are saying a thus saith the Lord--, sometimes especially if you are saying, *"Thus saith the Lord,"* you've got to be **sent by God**, and be wise in how you speak to avoid punishment or worse.

Politicians lie easily, it seems. They are contracted to do the will of the **power** that put them in power, albeit temporarily. In a democracy the people think "elected officials" are serving the people.

Nope.

The *people* didn't really put them in power, but they *think* they did. Well, the power that gave them favor in the eyes of the people did this thing for them. So now they do the John 10:10 all too easily; they steal, kill, and destroy according to their **assignments**. They owe this powerful power, and they must also continue to *pay to play*.

To be in power, but put there by occultic powers is a terrible thing; that man or woman is really not their own anymore. It is as though they have sold their soul. It's why folks start out so innocent and clean, but then seem to get corrupted once in office and never keep many or any of the shining promises they made to be elected.

All the while, the human powers behind the leaders continue to look innocent and guilt-free. They are usually very rich and give freely, and publicly to charitable foundations and organizations. The person they put in power takes the fall if something goes sideways, and the next guy who wants power or is greedy and willing to make a deal is up.

Next!

Unless God establishes the king in Righteousness that leader is owing to the default kingdoms of this world, the prince of this world is running this world. Do not be deceived or surprised.

Pray for your politicians and those in power because the Word says so. But, also pray for them because they have the authority to make your life good or bad, easier or more difficult. They have the authority and the ability to put policies in force that can make your children's lives easier or harder, even your *children's* children. The heart of the king is in the hands of the Lord; pray for your leaders no matter how good or bad they are.

Like the movie ***Ghostbusters***, the evil powers feed on evil. If you are evil, you will not make an evil power less wicked, no matter what you do, either in the spiritual realm or if you protest for a thousand days in the natural. They will become defensive and rebel and be even worse.

Be in Christ and stay prayerful.

Be wise. Do not blame your relatives, your neighbors, or co-workers if your life seems difficult, they are usually under far lower powers and lower altars than your governmental leaders. If not for yourself, pray for the sake of your generations.

**According to** the book, **When Evil Altars Are Multiplied, Overthrowing Evil Altars** by Dr. Prayer Madueke whose book inspired this one, *"Once you can deal with these two altars, River Altars and Astral Altars, ruled by the Queen of Heaven, then every other altar is minor."*

**Crossroad Altars** are found at four corner roads. There are a lot of those in this world. When demons are summoned at four corner roads the victims of such will never have rest and demons are constant and relentless, coming from all four directions, in turn, to waste a person's life. This altar type is very serious in its program of destruction.

# Mobile Altars

A person can go to an evil altar, or the altar can come to the person. As said, people can both move altars, and people can *be* altars. Other altars that come to a person are such as evil charms, beads, amulets, and animal altars.

**Roadkill is an altar.** Anything that has bloodshed has received a sacrifice and is an altar. Yes, you can feel for the poor animal that lost its life and even for the driver of the car that hit it, but without getting a persecution complex, think--, did your *familiar spirit* by chance report what you'd be doing today? Did it report what direction or what roads you might be driving on, or walking by? Evil animal altars, especially of dead animals are to DEFILE you. Before the enemy can properly curse you, you must be guilty, have iniquity, or be defiled.

A woman reported that one day, on her daily walk she encountered more than eight dead animals, not all in one place, but throughout her 2-mile journey. Those evil altars were in place to defile her because at that time she was under very heavy witchcraft attack and oppression, but was being very diligent to stay in the will of God and not sin. Without sin, iniquity, or defilement none of the witchcraft that was being sent her way could land on her or attach to her.

When you see a defiling evil altar, such as roadkill, pass it by. Pray. Do not lock eyes on it--, sometimes you can't *unsee* things. Obviously animal altars are mobile, well, at least until they die. There is no reason to have that stuck in your head. Right? Plead the Blood of Jesus and pray that that altar will have no negative effect over you, in the Name of Jesus.

A child of less than 10 years old had been worshipped by his father. The child was disciplined by his mother, and that's how the first marriage broke up. Because of the worship of the child, the father had turned the child into an evil altar. Yes, that child was a moving, breathing, living, mobile altar. The child quickly learned this at his level of immaturity learning how to work this inordinate favor from his father to his advantage. He was cute, did cute things, and garnered *more worship*.

All seemed right with that little world.

Until it wasn't.

The man remarried, and this child subsequently was turned against his new stepmother because he learned from his deceived father, and now understood that those who don't worship him and do everything he wants are problems. So, the kid one day told his stepmother that he was *cutting* the relationship between his dad and his new stepmother, who was nothing but loving toward the child. But, with his little fingers, he indicated the cutting like scissors cutting a string, cord, or rope. And that's how the second marriage broke up; that relationship was destroyed from that day.

Who taught that kid that? We don't know. Maybe he saw it on TV, perhaps it was in his blood and he automatically by *familiar spirits* knew how to do this--, since he had become an altar. Demons frequent evil altars. Well, we know it had access because the husband was worshipping an evil altar, so God was very limited in what could be done even for the second marriage.

Seasoned witches and warlocks can use pictures to destroy a marriage on evil altars, mobile or any other type. You should pray very well over personal items such as pictures, anything containing your DNA, even dirt tracked on the bottoms of your shoes or your car tires. A hair, a fingernail, a toenail, body fluids, your discarded, but worn clothing. I never thought I'd say this, but do not give your clothes away. Burn them. Your clothes can be used to create a covering cast, evil veil over you or curse you in some other way.

# This Is So Embarrassing

Of course, the power in any curse against a person is that the victim has an open door, iniquity, sin--, either their own, and or generational or ancestral iniquity. So, repent very well for your own sins, as well, then God has full rights to be in your life and protect you by His Spirit. Amen.

If an evil altar worker doesn't have a picture they may make an effigy, doll, or image to summon the spirit of their intended victim.

Let me say that this is so embarrassing--- for myself, as well as anyone that if your spirit is so weak, that your spiritual walls are so weak or non-existent that a witch can get to you and tear your life apart. Come on, the Greater One is in us--, well He is supposed to be.

How can a witch, or even a coven of witches overpower God?

It can't happen.

If a witch is overtaking you that means that you don't have enough God onboard--, or you don't have *any* God onboard to fight back spiritually. We do not war against flesh and blood so we need spiritual prowess to win over spiritual evil.

The Word says we wrestle against powers, rulers of darkness and spiritual wickedness in high places. Saints of God that means that greater gatherings than witches and warlocks may come against you, depending on who you are to God--, and that you will have to wrestle them. But we shall also prevail as long as we are in Christ. So prepare yourself, your warrior status will be tested in this life. Yes, worship the Lord, but at some time put down your harp and pick up your Sword.

Remember that *familiar spirit* or *monitoring spirit* that followed you home from the séance or whatever evil altar you went to, that you all did just for kicks? Yeah, that one. That evil *spirit* reported on you, having discovered the best day and the best way to attack you to steal, kill, bring you down, or destroy you. If you're not dead yet, that evil *spirit* is not going anywhere unless you **make** it leave. It is still gathering information for the next attack. If you are a prayerless, dry, cold "Christian," oh please, this is easy like drive through fast food, ***open all night.***

Awareness is necessary. Wise up. There are evil people and organizations out there looking to do any number of things to others, even against you. Just because you thought your powerful mind could protect you from witchcraft, by not believing in it. *Oh pls.* I've got more than one patient who doesn't believe that they have cavities because nothing hurts.

**Yet**.

But they have cavities. Some have a mouthful. These folks are coming to have a professional examine them and tell them about the condition of their mouth. No, *they* aren't they are coming to tell the professional about what they believe is the condition of their mouth, but that is what they are actually doing in this verbal exchange. Now, if the dentist agrees, does that make it so? No, it makes the dentist a liar and I won't be that.

So we argue.

Who will win?

If no dental fillngs are done, the cavities will win.

My point is, you'd better believe what is and not be in denial about truth. You're saved, *right?* Since you're saved, get the Holy Spirit as well so you can be led into all Truth. That is what the Holy Spirit does; it is one of His jobs.

Make sure that you are fully in Christ so you can have authority to speak to these demons, devils, altars and do spiritual warfare. You must be fully in, not halfway and not just on Sundays or the demons will laugh you out of town.

Jesus I know, Paul, I know, but who are you? That was New Testament.

And the evil spirit answered and said, Jesus I know, and Paul I know; but who are ye?
(Acts 19:15)

*What are we even talking about?* In Psalm 24 the gates that are commanded to be opened are talking back to the writer (David) and saying, Who is this King of Glory? If a Gate is going to talk smack about Jesus, asking Him who He is, what spiritual respect do you think a sometimey Christian will get? You must make yourself fully known in the spirit, in your Godly authority, in your position of dominion, and in spiritual warfare so you and God are not mocked.

Be well-versed in prayer. Stay prayed up. Be stable and not doubleminded. Be

HOT; do not be cold and especially don't be lukewarm. I beleive God is saying don't be hot + cold because that = lukewarm.

So you also are not embarrassed or embarrass God, sin not, as much as it is in you, by the Holy Spirit. Now to accomplish spiritual warfare:

1.  Repent for your own sins: Lord, have Mercy on me, a sinner. If I am none of Yours, give me a godly sorrow for my sins and a repentant heart, and make me one of Yours. Lord, forgive me of all my sins—sins of omission and commission, in the Name of Yeshua.
2.  Repent also for the sins of your parents and your ancestors, going back to or even before Adam and Eve.
3.  Make sure you are saved: I believe that Jesus is the Son of God and He came to Earth to save sin-sick man--, me, for we all have sinned and fallen short of the Glory of God.
4.  I believe that Jesus died and on the Third Day, God resurrected Him from

the dead, and He lives. Lord Jesus, come into my heart and BE the Lord of my life.

5. I put down all idols, in the Name of Jesus.

6. Lord, create in me a clean heart and renew a right spirit in me, in the Name of Jesus.

7. I confess my sins to You Lord, in the Name of Jesus.

8. Lord, forgive me. Today I ask You to help me forgive others, even 70 times 7, and also to forgive myself.

9. Lord, I forgive every **human** who's hurt me, betrayed me, embarrassed me, disappointed me, abandoned me, or let me down.

10. Vengeance is Yours, Lord, may any human who has hurt me, or sinned against me come to a saving knowledge of You, in the Name of Yeshua.

11. Lord, Jesus I dedicate my life to You; You are my Lord and Savior. Thank

You for saving me from myself and from Hell.

12. Teach me to walk in obedience and teach me to be in right standing with You, always, in the Name of Yeshua.

13. I need Your power, Your anointing, Your Grace to walk in Your ways to do Your Will, and to help grow the Kingdom of God, and to bear much good fruit, and fruit that remains, in the Name of Yeshua.

14. Jesus, thank You for who you are.

15. Baptize me now with the Holy Spirit and Fire, with the gift of tongues.

16. Holy Spirit, give me power to become an overcomer.

17. Holy Spirit, give me a drink of the new wine. Fill me up with Your Presence, fill me up with the Glory of God.

18. Thank You Jesus, for baptism with the Holy Spirit, with Fire and the gift of tongues.

*19.* And when He had said this, He breathed on them and said to them, ***Receive ye the Holy Ghost.***

20.Father, in the mighty Name of Jesus Christ please cover me, my thoughts, conscious and unconscious subconscious, the spirit, soul, body, emotions, and nervous systems, with the precious Blood of Jesus.

21.Precious Holy Spirit, You are the Spirit of liberty. You are the Spirit of Comfort. You are the Spirit of Truth, and You are the Spirit of Peace.

22.Holy Spirit help today. Be my Helper in this prayer and in deliverance, in the Name of Jesus.

23.Angels of God that guard the heirs of salvation. I have salvation through Christ Jesus. I release myself to be guarded by Your guardian angels. I am safe and heavily protected from all that seek to cause me harm and havoc, in the Name of Jesus.

# An Evil Clown

An evil (human) clown whom I knew too well--, and I say clown because after our friendship ended, the Lord showed me a dream where this man was as a court jester--, a clown. In the natural this person wanted me to send him many, many pictures of my business location. I did not, even though I hadn't had the clown dream of this jokester yet. He played playfully all the time so the average person may think he's an innocent, but silly man. He's not. He is wicked and working with wickedness for whatever rewards he is receiving from being as a *monitoring spirit* for his evil-co-agents. As a matter of fact, the Lord showed me, in the dream, this man carrying a ladder that he was trying to put away and hide before it could be seen by me, the dreamer. He was jovial and laughing the whole time.

A ladder in the dream can be good or bad. If it were good, then it might be as Jacob's ladder where an angel may descend from the Third Heaven and you can, like Jacob declare, *I won't let go until you bless me.*

If the ladder has a bad connotation, it might be in a setting such as I dreamed. The jester was in an medical clinic setting, but all the white doors to each treatment room had dirt on them. The clown in the dream was wearing tight suggestive clothing, laughing while quickly trying to take the ladder off screen as not to be seen. That was bad. Better prayer-treat that dream right away.

In Proverbs there is talk of steps that go down to hell; so we infer that ladders can go up or down depending on who has the ladder, who has authority to place or use the ladder or who has access points to reach a man by a ladder, by that man's permission, agreement, or iniquity.

Pictures are used maliciously by the dark altars unless they are prayed over very well. I didn't send any of my business office pictures, thank God. But if I had, or if you have, your prayer life can make you and everything that belongs to you too hot for these dark agents to use against you.

Pray without ceasing, so you can be hot!

**Tree altars** can lock up the life of a person, a family, or even a whole community. This looks like collective captivity, or the bondage suffered because of territorial powers.

Some cultures do evil sacrifices in fields, high places, forests. Their specialty is taking away blessings from others.

But an altar can look like anything and can be anywhere. Don't be surprised at what an altar might look like, or not look like. You could be looking at an altar in anyone's house; it could just look like décor.

This evil clown was someone that I knew in the natural. He was a mobile altar and that is an understatement; that man got around.

Of mobile altars, people can be evil altars—I say evil because they shouldn't be altars. Only the altar of Jesus Christ should be at work in the life of any saved person. But the evil altar that is requiring worship and/or emitting strange fire may be the cutest guy at the nightclub. She might be the finest lady there. Take a moment and think about this – you know.

You feel a certain way in their company, when they are around, like you've lost yourself or you want to lose yourself in them. That's a strange altar. Like you want to give yourself away to them--, you do realize that is selling your soul, or giving your soul away to someone or something that is not God, *right*?

So, even if this is your new *boo*, Baby, gather yourself, pull yourself together. No man, no woman should have this kind of power over you. See that you do not worship them or worship at their altar.

# Repent of Visiting Evil Altars

Folks, we have no idea what our parents, grandparents or ancestors did. Few will tell their secrets and will most often brag about any number of things that they take to their grave, while never revealing what those things are. If you think about it, the stink about it is the iniquity that is oozing or rising from graves that are enveloping bloodlines and ambushing innocent people. For this reason, we should repent for our own sins as well as for the sins of our ancestors. We need to pray for Mercy and ask the Lord to remove the iniquity of the bloodline that is causing grief, pain, affliction, and loss for us now in our own lives.

And they went out, and preached that men should repent. (Mark 6:12)

Jesus said, *"Repent for the Kingdom of Heaven is at hand."*

From that time Jesus began to preach, and to say, Repent: for the kingdom of heaven is at hand. (Matthew 4:17)

Father, in the Name of Jesus, I repent for my own sins, and I repent *for* my parents and my ancestors of all of the following:

1. Visiting evil altars at any time, for any reason, in the Name of Jesus.
2. I renounce and denounce the sin of having visited any evil altar at any time, in the Name of Jesus.

3. Lord, remove the iniquity from me and my bloodline, in the Name of Jesus.
4. Lord, break the curse created by the evil covenants made in this sin, in the Name of Jesus.
5. Father, I bind and paralyze every demon, devil, strongman or wickedness in place to enforce the curse in my life and bloodline, in the Name of Jesus.
6. Lord, break, dismantle, destroy every bondage and yoke because of these covenants and generational curses, in the Name of Jesus.

# *IF* They Did Any of This

7. Lord, I renounce and denounce and repent for myself and my parents and ancestors for going to evil altars: **IF THEY DID ANY OF THIS:** If they went to an evil altar of any kind:

8. To discover people's destinies and waste them.
9. To afflict, oppress, or destroy people's stars.

10. To influence people to make wrong decisions.
11. To capture and/or destroy the progress of others.
12. To bury the greatness of another person.
13. To seek evil power, spiritually.
14. To seek evil power, financially.
15. To seek evil power, politically.
16. To seek evil power, socially.
17. To uncover the nakedness of another person or people.
18. To fire evil arrows on another person's health.
19. To fire evil arrows at another person's business.
20. To fire evil arrows on another person's marriage, family, or other relationships.
21. To mark another person for rejection, hatred, disfavor, or reproach.
22. To close doors of opportunities for others.
23. To wear people out in life, make them tired, weary.
24. To make people give up in life, even on good and promising projects.

25. To send arrows of affliction.
26. To send arrows of death.
27. To lead another into error. To make them look for help in the wrong places.
28. To cause confusion in a person.
29. To cause lust and worldliness in a person.
30. To cause divorce in another's marriage.
31. To cause confusion, division, and worldliness in the Church.
32. To cause sin in a person, or in the Church.
33. To cause people to reject God and to reject holiness.

# Or This

34. To interfere with the blessings of God's people.
35. To promote hatred and division within the Church.
36. To send arrows of torment.
37. To send arrows of sorrows.
38. To cause others to struggle in profitless hard work.
39. To kill people's joy.
40. To send arrows of backsliding.
41. To divert the efforts of other's – steal from them.
42. To send arrows at the head or brain of a person.
43. To disgrace the people of God.
44. To humiliate the people of God.
45. To mock the people of God; to mock God.
46. To send arrows of failure.
47. To send arrows of disappointment.
48. To send arrows of discouragement.
49. To send arrows of depression.

50. To send arrows of suicide and suicidal thoughts to a person.
51. To send overwhelming grief into a person's life.
52. To send overwhelming desire for death into a person's life.
53. To send overwhelming lust into a person's life.
54. To send overwhelming desire to leave a person's marriage.
55. To send overwhelming fear into a person's life.
56. To send Tokoloshe or *spirit spouse* into a person's life.
57. To keep people into a spiritual marriage.

58. To send people into the wrong profession in life.
59. To jump someone into an evil timeline.

# Also Repent of This

60. To send a spirit of dissension and quarreling into a home. To yoke people with heavy problems.
61. To yoke people with cyclical, seasonal problems.
62. To send poverty to another person, or people.
63. To send arrows of untimely death.
64. To send hopelessness into another's life.
65. To keep people in evil relationships.
66. To keep people in the yokes and bondages of curses.

67. To send a covering cast.
68. To send anti-pregnancy arrows.
69. To send arrows of miscarriage.
70. To steal the promotion of others.
71. To send witchcraft arrows that bewitch people to get them under your control.
72. To cause people to miss divine connections.
73. To cause people to meet the wrong people in life.
74. To send arrows of foundation pollution.
75. To send arrows that send people into sin.

76. To send arrows that send people to hell.
77. To learn their future or their fortune.
78. To get the attention of a certain girl or boy, lady or man.
79. To get a spouse.
80. To get a child or children.
81. To win in the contest – be it a game, a business deal or other bid.
82. To defeat an enemy or a perceived enemy.
83. To learn any kind of occultic or psychic knowledge.
84. To knock someone else out of the running for something you want to earn or win.

# And This

85. To get your crops to grow.
86. For a rich harvest of cattle.
87. To be fruitful in hunting for food for family.
88. To be successful in fishing for food for family or to take to market.
89. To hinder someone else's success at hunting or fishing.
90. To be better than your sibling.
91. To be better than your neighbor.

92. So your kids will be better than their kids.
93. To better your spouse, so they will have more or be richer, for example.
94. To have a better house or car, better clothes.
95. To issue beauty curses and anti-beauty arrows against someone else.
96. To cause someone else to lose – anything at all, just have them to lose.

The reason you must do this is that you should repent. You must repent. But saints of God listen up, what you are experiencing may or may not be because evil altars are emanating at you, or that evil arrows are actively being sent against you. This could be the return of evil arrows that you, yourself, in your evil, unforgiveness, bitterness have sent out and they didn't hit a godly target, so they are coming back on you. **So, you'd better repent.**

What's coming at you could be what your parents or other ancestors sent out and they also didn't hit, couldn't hit a prayed up, prayerful one, so they are coming back on your bloodline. It may be 100 years later, so now you are identified as the "person" of interest, as either the person who sent it out, or the blood relative (child) of the person who sent a failed arrow out, because the blood in you matches the blood of the person who sent it.

The evil covenant that was made to allow those arrows to be sent out was made in blood. It was made in your blood, possibly years and years ago before you were ever formed or born, somebody signed your name, by signing in your blood because they have the same blood.

# I Was Only Kidding

Even if you didn't believe in the evil altar but you went anyway just to see what would happen, what would happen, happened. You still need to repent.

97. Lord, I repent of seeking out or using Tarot cards or seeking out readers to know the future, or any other ungodly thing by psychic means. I repent for my parents and ancestors of the same, in the Name of Jesus.
98. Lord, I repent of looking at, reading, seeking out, believing or acting on horoscopes; I repent for my parents and ancestors as well, in the Name of Jesus.
99. Father, I repent of looking at astrology to know any information that I should be getting from You. I

repent also for my parents and ancestors, in the Name of Jesus.

100.     Lord, I repent of seeking fortune tellers at the beach or anywhere, even if it was just for fun, in the Name of Jesus.

101.     Lord, I repent of going to or participating in seances, necromancy, or any summoning the dead, for any reason, in the Name of Jesus.

102.     Lord, forgive my parents and ancestors of the same, in the Name of Jesus.

103.     Lord I repent of yoga, martial arts or any art or movement form where idols are invoked and bowed to or worshipped. Lord, forgive my parents and ancestors of the same, in the Name of Jesus.

104.     Lord forgive me for believing in or using crystals and any other form of New Ageism, and forgive my parents and ancestors of the same if they have done this, in the Name of Jesus.

105.     Lord, forgive me and my bloodline of divination, tea readings,

coffee readings, runes, bones, even animal intestines to know the future, in the Name of Jesus.

106.    Lord, forgive me of looking at or believing in Angel Numbers, Numerology, or Angel Worship as none of that is of You. Also forgive my parents and ancestors if they have done the same, in the Name of Jesus.

107.    Lord, forgive me for worshipping "saints" especially in Catholicism since they are repackaged pagan *gods* from Africa and are not really saints at all. Father, also forgive my parents and ancestors for the same, in the Name of Jesus.

108.    I repent for all other forms of idolatry, in the Name of Jesus.

109.    I repent Lord, I really didn't mean it. I didn't mean anything by it. I thought it was just for fun. I was just doing what everyone else was doing, but now I know better.

110.    I repent of raffles and gambling and worshipping at the altar of any strange or idol *god*, who lord over games of chance and that have made

false and counterfeit promises. I repent also for my parents and ancestors if they ever did the same, in the Name of Jesus.

# But I Was Just a Child

111.    Lord, forgive me of childish endeavors, whether I was saved or not, but I just didn't know any better.

Childhood witchcraft or occult games such as 8-Ball. Forgive me and my parents and ancestors, in the Name of Jesus.

112.     When I was a child, I thought as a child. Lord, forgive my childhood vows, oaths, promises, and sins, my childhood ignorance and folly, and also forgive all the sins of the early and childhood days of my parents and ancestors, in the Name of Jesus.

113.     I repent of using an Ouija Board, any necromancy or attempting to talk to the dead. Lord, forgive my parents and ancestors if they've ever done the same, in the Name of Jesus.

114.     Lord, forgive me for participating in holidays and festivals of demons or idols, such as Halloween. Lord, forgive my parents and ancestors if they've ever done the same.

115.     Lord, forgive me for participating in pagan holidays, knowingly or unknowingly. Forgive

my parents and ancestors if they ever did the same, in the Name of Jesus.

116.     Lord, forgive me of childhood vows and oaths that may have formed evil covenants and brought curses into my life or bloodline. Forgive also my parents and ancestors of the same, in the Name of Jesus.

# But He Was So Cute

She turned that guy into a whole idol. Some years ago, a woman was rejected by a love interest. She came home to her country porch sat in a rocking chair and rocked herself crazy. That is at least how the story is told in that family.

He lost himself in that girl because she had this, that, or the other and he never thought he could *pull* a girl like that.

117.     Lord forgive me of idolatry. Lord, forgive me for relationship idolatry. Lord, forgive me for sexual idolatry. Forgive my parents and ancestors if they've ever done the same, in the Name of Jesus.

118.     Lord, forgive me of worshipping a person.

119.     Lord, forgive me of lusting for a person to the degree that I would deny You or go around You to get them by any means. Forgive my parents and ancestors if they've ever done the same, and remove all iniquity from our bloodline, in the Name of Jesus.

120.     Lord, forgive me for pornography, or visiting evil altars of lust, fornication, adultery and other sexual idolatry, in the Name of Jesus. Lord, forgive my parents and ancestors if they have ever done the same.

121.     Lord, forgive me for coveting the spouse of my neighbor or the

spouse of a stranger, in the Name of Jesus. Father, forgive both my parents and all my ancestors if they have done similarly and incurred a curse on this family's bloodline, in the Name of Jesus.

122.     Forgive me of seeking the dark kingdom to find out what they were doing, where they were and how to win their affections.

123.     Forgive me of love potions, love spells of any kind. Forgive my parents and ancestors if they've ever done the same, in the Name of Jesus.

124.     Lord, forgive me of any form of witchcraft, manipulation, control, or trickery to trap a person into a relationship. Forgive my parents or ancestors if they did such a thing, in the Name of Jesus.

125.     Lord, cleanse me if I am the product of such a manipulated witchcraft relationship.

126.     Lord, cleanse me if there are dark things surrounding my

conception and birth that may be contributing to why my life is like it is, in the Name of Jesus.

127.    Lord, forgive my parents and ancestors if they have brought any curse to me or our bloodline because of conception rituals at evil altars, in the Name of Jesus.

128.    Lord, forgive me if I have worshipped at any strange or evil altar for any reason, in the Name of Jesus.

129.    Lord, forgive my parents and ancestors if they have worshipped at any strange or evil altar and have invited *familiar spirits, monitoring spirits* and devils into our family that is now affecting our bloodline, in the Name of Jesus.

# I Couldn't Help Myself

Excuses and lame explanations do not lead to repentance.

Desperation for anything may lead you to an evil altar or draw the evil altar to you. Ever notice how things that tempt you or interrupt what you are planning to do for God or for holiness just seem to show up right after you've made up your mind to serve the Lord more seriously?

130.     Lord, forgive me of lame excuses and for being too prideful to repent, in the Name of Jesus.

131.     Lord, forgive me for desperation and not putting my trust in You; forgive my parents and ancestors for the same, in the Name of Jesus.

132.	Lord, forgive me for yielding to temptation where I just couldn't help myself. Forgive my parents and ancestors if they ever found themselves in a similar situation, in the Name of Jesus.

# Trickery

If I, my parents, or any of my ancestors were tricked into going to an evil altar, or if an evil altar came to them, as to ambush them, Lord, forgive me and my family line for spiritual ignorance. Your Word says that You would not have us ignorant…

The serpent was an evil, mobile animal altar and it came into the Garden to Eve.

133.  Lord, forgive me for lacking knowledge and forgive my parents and ancestors for the same, so that our bloodline does not perish, in the Name of Jesus.

134.  Lord, forgive me, my parents, and my ancestors for lacking discernment and not using the

spiritual gifts that You have made available for us, so we would escape temptation, in the Name of Jesus.

# Forgetfulness

Man has a tendency to forget. Since all the ways of a man are clean in his own eyes, man especially forgets the wrongs that he has done. So even if a man, especially a parent, *forgets* all of their wrong as they now vow to do better, to do right, or suddenly want to set a good example for their own children, they may forget the sins of their own youth. They may even forget the sins they committed yesterday. Just yesterday. Some people think just stopping a behavior is all that is needed to make all the issues that go with that sinful behavior also stop.

Nope.

Because of the sin and because evil covenants were made--, those covenants were made in blood. God doesn't look too kindly on breaking covenants, and how do you as a human, in your flesh expect to stop a demon that is coming to enforce a curse that is the result of an evil covenant that may have a *forever* clause in it?

The only way is if GOD breaks the covenant and forgets it, Himself. Your just forgetting it doesn't do much of anything except get you into more trouble.

Behold, for peace I had great bitterness: but thou hast in love to my soul *delivered it* from the pit of corruption: for thou hast cast all my sins behind thy back. (Isaiah 38:17)

**You** can't stop a speeding train by simply standing on the railroad tracks unless the conductor sees you, wants to stop, has time to stop and can stop. You also can't stop the speeding train by simply getting off the railroad tracks either. Some **force** of some kind has to be applied.

A demon doesn't have any desire to stop. They have to be made to stop and that will take Jesus Christ, spiritual warfare, the Blood of Jesus, and combinations of warfare verbiage, decrees, declarations, repentance, renunciation, denunciations, et cetera. It's doable, but it can get complicated. It takes force.

> And from the days of John the Baptist until now the kingdom of heaven suffereth violence, and the violent take it by force.
> (Matthew 11:12)

Oh, saints of God, it is so much easier to walk circumspectly and never enter into evil covenants, than to get out of them. But there is no condemnation here, we all have sinned and fallen short of the Glory of God.

This ancestor of yours may forgive themselves, and consider all the wrong they did forgotten and over with because they did the sin only once, or have since stopped the behavior.

The blood that they made one or more evil covenants with is still speaking. The blood on the altar is still speaking, and that's why the altar is still emanating against your bloodline. Your parents may or may not feel relief, but the altar is still there.

The virus that makes a person have a cold takes 2 to 3 days to incubate. The virus is in there on Monday, but if the immune system doesn't rise up to defeat it, by Thursday someone will be blowing their nose.

Spiritual warfare is the spiritual immune response to get what is already acting out, or is in you and your bloodline, incubating, waiting to attack you, out of your system for good. Else, it's only a matter of time before somebody's spiritual nose will be runny or stuffy, or both. Or worse, that spiritual nose could get bloody if the non-repentant get a spiritual beat down. Covenants are certainly all about time. Always.

Your parents and ancestors may mean well and may do all that forgiving but forget to repent. This is the *why* of this book. We must always repent, and we must also repent for our parents and our ancestors. We have that authority and that responsibility.

Repentance can be, Lord, forgive me for all my sins, forgive me for sins of omission and commission. Or, more thoroughly we can repent for everything , line upon line, and sin upon sin. In my humble opinion, as detailed as you can be in your repentance regarding visiting evil altars, the sooner you will put the entire sin and iniquity to rest, in the Name of Jesus.

# Fake Churches

There are plenty of folks that make their living and make it their business to blow the whistle on churches or pastors that they believe are fakes. I'm not called to do that.

There are also evil altars at fake churches. How can you tell if a church is fake? Ask God. There are false pastors, false prophets aplenty. If the altar at your church is not a proper interface to the Spirit of God, then you will need to pray diligently so the Holy Spirit can advise you.

Trusting that every building with a steeple or a cross is of God and has been planted by God, is sanctioned and ordained by God is a big jump. What you may have been initiated into or what may have been taken from you or transferred from you at a false altar is for the Lord to reveal to you through His Holy Spirit.

Hopefully, you, your parents or your ancestors didn't go to a fake church altar knowingly, but the spiritual fallout from having gone to that altar, agreed with that altar, given offerings of money, worship, or time on that altar still constituted an evil covenant.

Remember, covenants are made and forged in blood and unless they are broken with their associated curses, **by a higher altar**, they will continue on into the generations.

Be sure to repent for your own mistakes and sins, as well as those of your parents and ancestors.

# Sent

Please know that things are different if you've been **_sent_** by God to a certain place, even if that place has an evil altar or is the place of an evil altar.

If God has sent you, you are covered and protected from any projections or emanations from the evil altar. In other words, God sent you, you did not send yourself, so you are covered. You are covered because the one who sent you is greater than the one He *sent*.

Even if multiple altars are built or increased right in front of your face, if God is with you, if God has sent you, you have no problem. When Elisha defeated 450 prophets of Baal on Mount Carmel, e was one prophet of God, who was sent so he had full spiritual coverage.

Even if altars are hidden and you don't even know they are there, but the Lord sent you, again you have no problems.

If altars are from household wickedness and the Lord has sent you, you shall prevail. God sent Gideon to tear down the evil altars that his father had erected, those altars didn't hurt Gideon, but he was victorious in what he was sent to do.

You also can be victorious.

First, repent.

**AMEN.**

## Dear Reader

Thank you for acquiring, reading, and praying this prayerbook. I pray that it has set you and your bloodline free of the iniquity of visiting or attending to evil altars.

In the Name of Jesus,

**Amen.**

Dr. Marlene Miles

# Prayer books by this author

While most books by this author have prayer points either throughout the book or at the end, there are some books that are **only** prayers. You just open up the book and pray. They are listed below:

**Prayers Against Barrenness:** *For Success in Business and Life*

**Fruit of the Womb:** *Prayers Against Barrenness*

**Beauty Curses,** *Warfare Prayers Against*
https://a.co/d/5Xlc20M

**Courts of Marriage: Prayers for Marriage in the Courts of Heaven** *(prayerbook)*
https://a.co/d/cNAdgAq

## Courtroom Warfare @ Midnight *(prayerbook)*
https://a.co/d/5fc7Qdp

## Demonic Cobwebs *(prayerbook)* https://a.co/d/fp9Oa2H

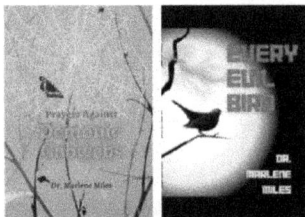

## Every Evil Bird https://a.co/d/hF1kh1O

## Every Evil Arrow https://a.co/d/afgRkiA

## Gates of Thanksgiving

## Spirits of Death & the Grave, Pass Over Me and My House https://a.co/d/dS4ewyr

*Please note that my name is spelled incorrectly on amazon, but not on the book.*

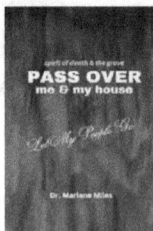

Throne of Grace: Courtroom Prayer

https://a.co/d/fNMxcM9

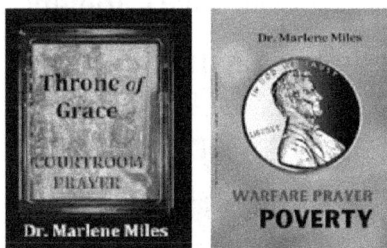

Warfare Prayer Against Poverty
https://a.co/d/bZ611Yu

# Other books by this author

AK: *The Adventures of the Agape Kid*

AMONG SOME THIEVES

Ancestral Powers https://a.co/d/9prTyFf

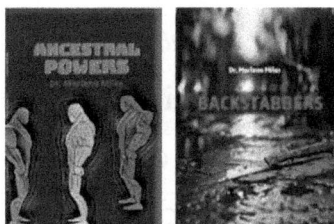

Backstabbers https://a.co/d/gi8iBxf

Barrenness, *Prayers Against*
https://a.co/d/feUltIs

Battlefield of Marriage, *The*

Blindsided: *Has the Old Man Bewitched You?*
https://a.co/d/5O2fLLR

Break Free from Collective Captivity

Casting Down Imaginations
https://a.co/d/1UxlLqa

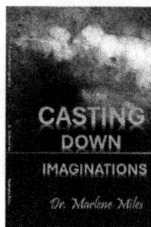

Churchzilla, The Wanna-Be, Supposed-to-be Bride of Christ

Curses of Blind Men

Demonic Cobwebs (prayerbook)

Demonic Time Bombs

Demons Hate Questions

Devil Loves Trauma, *The*

Devil Weapons: Unforgiveness, Bitterness,...

The Devourers: Thieves of Darkness 2

Do Not Swear by the Moon

Don't Refuse Me, Lord (4 book series)

https://a.co/d/idP34LG

Dream Defilement

The Emptiers: *Thieves of Darkness, 1*
https://a.co/d/5I4n5mc

Every Evil Arrow https://a.co/d/afgRkiA

Evil Touch https://a.co/d/gSGGpS1

Failed Assignment https://a.co/d/3CXtjZY

Fantasy Spirit Spouse https://a.co/d/hW7oYbX

FAT Demons (The): *Breaking Demonic Curses*

The Fold (5-book series)

- The Fold (Book 1)
- Name Your Seed (Book 2)
- The Poor Attitudes of Money (3)
- Do Not Orphan Your Seed (4)
- For the Sake of the Gospel (5)
- My Sowing Journal

Gang Ups: Touch Not God's Anointed

got HEALING? Verses for Life

got LOVE? Verses for Life

got HOPE? Verses for Life

got money? https://a.co/d/g2av41N

How to Dental Assist

How to Dental Assist2: Be Productive, Not Wasteful

I Take It Back

Legacy

Let Me Have A Dollar's Worth
https://a.co/d/h8F8XgE

Level the Playing Field

Living for the NOW of God

Lose My Location https://a.co/d/crD6mV9

Man Safari, *The*

Marriage Ed. Rules of Engagement & Marriage

Made Perfect in Love

Money Hunters: Beware of Those

Money on the Altar https://a.co/d/4EqJ2Nr

Mulberry Tree https://a.co/d/9nR9rRb

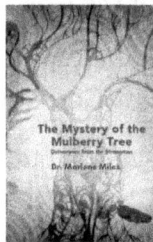

The Mystery of the
Mulberry Tree

Dr. Marlene Miles

Motherboard (The) - *Soul Prosperity Series*

Name Your Seed

Occupy: *Until I Return*

Plantation Souls

Players Gonna Play

Power Money: Nine Times the Tithe

https://a.co/d/gRt41gy

The Power of Wealth *(forthcoming)*

Powers Above

Repent of Visiting Evil Altars
https://a.co/d/3n3Zjwx

The Robe, Part 1, The Lessons of Joseph

The Robe, Part II, The Lessons of Joseph

Seasons of Grief

Seasons of Waiting

Seasons of War

Second Marriage, Third--, *Any Marriage*

https://a.co/d/6m6GN4N

Sift You Like Wheat

Six Men Short: What Has Happened to all the Men?

Soul Prosperity soul prosperity series 3

https://a.co/d/5p8YvCN

Souls Captivity soul prosperity series 2

The Spirit of Poverty

StarStruck

SUNBLOCK

The Swallowers: *Thieves of Darkness,* 3

Take It Back

This Is NOT That: How to Keep Demons from Coming at You

Time Is of the Essence

Too Many Wives: *Why You Have Lady Problems*

Tormenting Spirits   https://a.co/d/dAogEJf

Toxic Souls

Triangular Power *(series)*

- Powers Above
- SUNBLOCK
- Do Not Swear by the Moon
- STARSTRUCK

Uncontested Doom

Unguarded Hours, *The*

Unseen Life, *The* https://a.co/d/0drZ5Ll

Upgrade: How to Get Out of Survival Mode

- Toxic Souls (Book 2 of series)
- Legacy (Book 3 of series)

## The Wasters: *Thieves of Darkness*, Bk 2

https://a.co/d/bUvI9Jo

## What Have You to Declare? What Do You Have With You from Where You've Been?

## When I Was A Child, *I Prayed As a Child*

## When the Devourer is Rebuked

https://a.co/d/1HVv8oq

**The Wilderness Romance *(series)*** This series is about conducting a Godly relationship and marriage with someone who is a Wilderness person. It is about how to recognize it and navigate through it. These books are about how not to get caught up in such.

- *The Social Wilderness*
- *The Sexual Wilderness*
- *The Spiritual Wilderness*

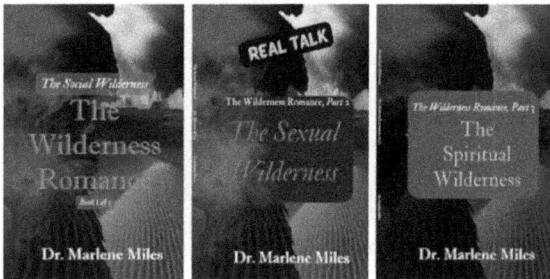

# Other Series

## The Fold (a series on Godly finances)
https://a.co/d/4hz3unj

**Soul Prosperity Series** https://a.co/d/bz2M42q

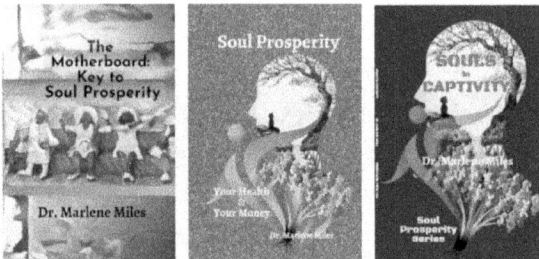

## Spirit Spouse books

https://a.co/d/9VehDSo

https://a.co/d/97sKOwm

## Thieves of Darkness series

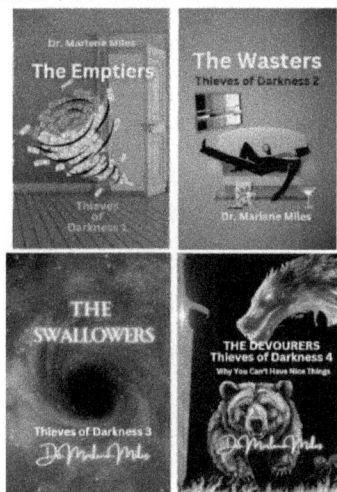

**Triangular Powers** https://a.co/d/aUCjAWC

**Upgrade** (series) *How to Get Out of Survival Mode*
https://a.co/d/aTERhX0

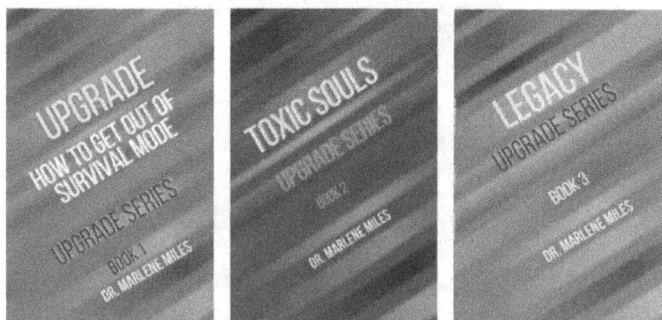

www.ingramcontent.com/pod-product-compliance
Lightning Source LLC
Chambersburg PA
CBHW062002040426
42447CB00010B/1874